Ian's Show and Tell Surprise:
A Story About Autism Spectrum Disorder

Written by: Vicenta Montgomery

Illustrated by: Christopher-James Bolognese-Warrington

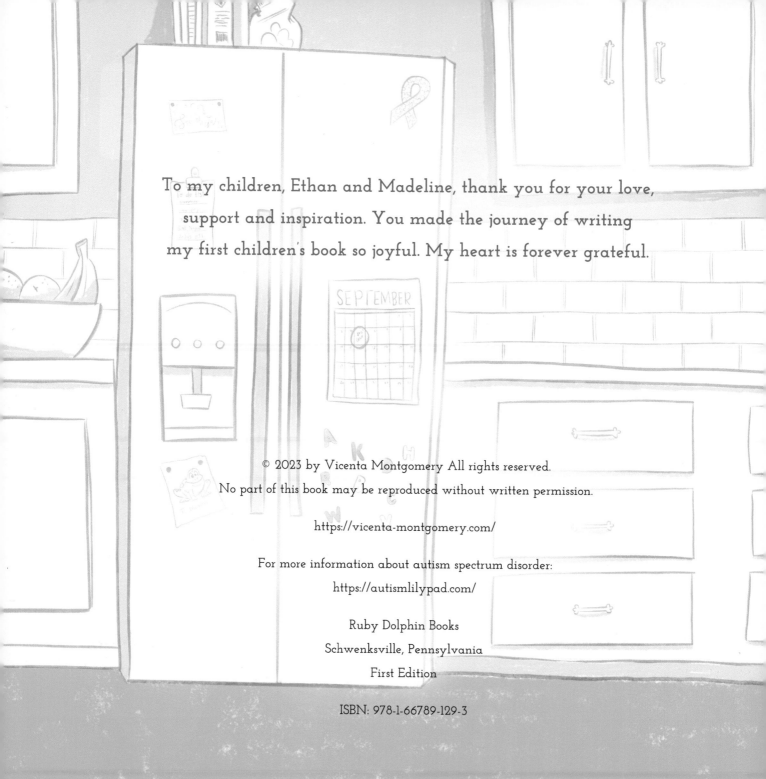

To my children, Ethan and Madeline, thank you for your love,
support and inspiration. You made the journey of writing
my first children's book so joyful. My heart is forever grateful.

https://vicenta-montgomery.com/

For more information about autism spectrum disorder:

https://autismlilypad.com/

Ruby Dolphin Books

Schwenksville, Pennsylvania

First Edition

ISBN: 978-1-66789-129-3

Ian was looking forward to the beginning of a new school year.

"I can't wait to start third grade.
It's gonna be great!"
he announced to his mom.

Ian enjoyed learning, going to class,
and playing outside just like everybody else.

However, Ian did things a **little differently** at times.
Like when he would cover his ears during indoor recess.

Playing musical chairs was fun to most kids,
but not to him.

At the Halloween party, there was a plate of yummy cupcakes with tons of icing. When it was Ian's turn to get one, **he froze**. "Just grab one, Ian," a student behind him called out.

He didn't realize that Ian was afraid of getting icing all over his hands. That was finger-licking deliciousness to most kids, but not Ian.

While in line for pictures, Ian was standing too close to the girl in front of him. She turned around and gave him a 'could you back up' kind of look. But Ian didn't get the message. She, like the rest of the class, didn't know that Ian did not understand communication without the words.

Ian often found himself playing alone.

One night Ian confessed to his mom, "I don't play with anyone at recess."

"Why not?" his mom asked.

Ian frowned, "I don't know how to join them.

"I know you will figure something out, sweetie," she replied.

The next day, Ian saw kids run by playing cops and robbers.

"Hi," he said softly.

No one noticed.

Ian walked over to a couple of kids playing hopscotch.

"That looks fun." The words barely came out.

Again, nothing. They just kept playing.

Ian felt left out. *How do I get them to understand that I want to play?* he wondered.

Following recess, the teacher announced,
"Next Tuesday will be **Show and Tell.**"
The teacher quickly added,
"Please no pets. Last year was a mess."

After dinner that night, Ian looked around his room with his favorite stuffy and asked "What should I bring to Show and Tell, Froggy? Maybe I could bring my karate belt or my guitar."

Then, Ian started to think about how he didn't feel connected to the other students. "I wish they understood me the way you do, Froggy," he sighed.

Suddenly, an idea popped into his head.
"**I can talk about me!** I'll tell them about autism and show them how I think differently. Then they'll understand."

Unable to control his excitement, he ran into his parents' bedroom and shouted, "I'm going to teach my class about autism!"

"**That's a great idea,**" Ian's Dad cheered.

It was like Ian slipped into superhero mode and was ready to teach the world.

"Mom, can you go with me to find things to help explain my differences?"

Delighted, mom said, "**Of course. Let's go!**"

They dug through his room,
his closet, and even the play room
to gather all kinds of things.

On the morning of Show and Tell, Ian could feel his breakfast grumbling in his tummy. *Will I be able to explain it all? Are they going to laugh?* So many things raced through his head as he watched others share.

Finally, it was Ian's turn. With his heart doing cartwheels underneath his shirt, he dragged a giant bag to the front of the class.

"I have a surprise for Show and Tell: I have lots of things to Show because I want to Tell you about autism spectrum disorder. Also known as ASD or just autism." Not sure what this was all about, the students leaned forward to get a better look.

"First, this is **my best stuffy Froggy**. He accepts me just the way I am even when I do something unexpected. I hope you will do the same." Ian put on a pair of sunglasses. "I often talk to friends without looking at them. I don't notice changes in your face that would normally tell someone else if you are mad or sad. I need you to tell me how you are feeling if you want to be sure I understand."

Next, he held a hula hoop over his head and let it drop to the floor. "I might need a reminder to not stand too close to you when we are in line together...unless you want to draw a big circle around yourself every day." He was relieved when he got a little laughter from the class.

Ian dove back into the bag to get some smaller items from the bottom.

"I may have a fidget toy in my hand because it can be difficult to sit still. And just like this yo-yo, I might repeat a movement with my body or even repeat a sentence over and over and not realize it."

Ian put on a raincoat, headphones and a pair of gloves and explained,

"There are some things that bother me that may not bother you. Loud noises, flashing lights, getting my hands messy, or even getting rained on can make me feel nervous. It is the way I was born, just like the color of my eyes or the color of my hair. My brain receives these things differently. When these things happen, I may need time to recover, but I'll be okay."

Next, Ian pulled a road sign out of the bag. "When our regular schedule takes a turn, I might get worried and need a moment to adjust."
Ian was on a roll.

"This might be hard for you to understand but making friends doesn't come naturally to me. To help explain, I have a little experiment for you. I will need a volunteer." Ian was thrilled to see that everyone raised a hand to participate.

Ian placed a toy train engine and a caboose on the desk of one of the students and asked, "Will you connect them together please?"

Looking puzzled, the student said,
"But they don't work together like that. You need to turn one around."

"Exactly" Ian exclaimed. "The train pieces don't connect unless you line them up right. They need help to join each other. I have a social skills teacher who helps me learn how to join my classmates in ordinary activities. Such as taking turns during play time, making eye contact when I speak, and giving others a chance to share their thoughts."

The captivated class waited to see if Ian would pull anything else out of the bag. He reached in and pulled out a banner ...

"One of my superpowers is attention to detail, which can make me pretty handy to have around. I hope you liked learning about autism. I would love to learn what makes you different and special too!"

Ian peeked over his sunglasses
and was so happy to see a room
filled with smiles and cheers.

When they lined up for the buses that afternoon,
Ian was standing too close to the girl in front of him.
She turned around and whispered, "Ian...hula hoop...remember?"
It worked! Ian took a step back and was beaming with pride.

The next day at recess, a classmate noticed Ian standing nearby,

"Hey Ian, wanna try jump rope?"

"Sure!" Ian replied. **Ian was part of the fun**. It was just that easy.

You could almost see his superhero cape flapping in the breeze.

After school that day, Ian had a surprise for his parents.
"Guess what?" Ian said, grinning from ear to ear.

"Someone asked me to play with them
on the playground today. We had such
a great time and you know what...
it really is gonna be **a great year!**"

WANT TO LEARN MORE?

Autism Spectrum Disorder, or ASD, is a term applied to a wide variety of symptoms that can be expressed very differently from one child to another. Children with ASD are boys or girls who look just like you and me but may act in an unexpected way from time to time.

The way a child with ASD communicates, thinks, or develops problem-solving abilities ranges greatly from children who are gifted learners to those that are severely challenged. Children with ASD may speak freely or may be non-verbal. Each child is different and will require different types of support in their daily lives.

The American Academy of Pediatrics described ASD as a common neurodevelopmental disorder characterized by social and communication impairment and restricted or repetitive behaviors.
https://www.aappublications.org/news/2019/12/16/autism121619

The Center for Disease Control and Prevention describes ASD as a developmental disability that can cause significant social, communication, and behavioral challenges. In a surveillance program performed in 2018, the CDC reported the overall prevalence and characteristics of ASD among children aged 8 years to be about one in 44. For more information about the surveillance methods and locations used for the report, please go to the website noted below or cdc.gov and search the Autism and Developmental Disabilities Monitoring (ADDM) Network.
https://www.cdc.gov/mmwr/volumes/70/ss/ss7011a1.htm?s_cid=ss7011a1_w

Both websites contain much more information about screening and diagnosis for ASD and are great places to start to learn more.

A Note from the Author

This book was inspired by my son's bravery when he was in the third grade and stood in front of his class to give them a presentation about himself and his journey with autism spectrum disorder. I was so proud of him, and I saw how much it helped others in his class understand him better. My hope is that this book can be shared in classrooms everywhere to help children understand differences that they may encounter in their peers' behavior and feel safe to ask questions rather than avoid the child who seems "different" to them.

Sometimes just a little understanding can provide the acceptance that every child deserves, no matter his or her differences. I also created the website AutismLilypad.com  (https://www.autismlilypad.com) as a place to find resources that may be helpful for a parent/caregiver of a child suspected of having or diagnosed with autism spectrum disorder. A percentage of the proceeds from the sale of this book will go towards providing copies to elementary school libraries across the country and eventually the world. Thank you for your purchase and for sharing in the process of improving awareness acceptance for neurodiverse children everywhere.

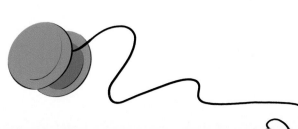